THE MAN IN THE IRON MASK
[An Essay]

*(This is the essay entitled
The Man in the Iron Mask, not the novel
"The Man in the Iron Mask")*

by

Alexandre Dumas

Copyright © 2012 Read Books Ltd.
This book is copyright and may not be
reproduced or copied in any way without
the express permission of the publisher in writing

British Library Cataloguing-in-Publication Data
A catalogue record for this book is available from the
British Library

Alexandre Dumas

Alexandre Dumas was born in Villers-Cotterêts, France in 1802. His parents were poor, but their heritage and good reputation – Alexandre's father had been a general in Napoleon's army – provided Alexandre with opportunities for good employment. In 1822, Dumas moved to Paris to work for future king Louis Philippe I in the Palais Royal. It was here that he began to write for magazines and the theatre.

In 1829 and 1830 respectively, Dumas produced the plays Henry III and His Court and Christine, both of which met with critical acclaim and financial success. As a result, he was able to commit himself full-time to writing. Despite the turbulent economic times which followed the Revolution of 1830, Dumas turned out to have something of an entrepreneurial streak, and did well for himself in this decade. He founded a production studio that turned out hundreds of stories under his creative direction, and began to produce serialised novels for newspapers which were widely read by the French public. It was over the next two decades, as a now famous and much loved author of romantic and adventuring sagas, that Dumas produced his best-known works – the D'Artagnan romances, including The Three Musketeers, in 1844, and The Count of Monte Cristo, in 1846.

Dumas made a lot of money from his writing, but he was almost constantly penniless as a result of his extravagant lifestyle and love of women. In 1851 he fled his creditors to Belgium, and then Russia, and then Italy, not returning to Paris until 1864. Dumas died in Puys, France, in 1870, at the age of 68. He is now enshrined in the Panthéon of Paris alongside fellow authors Victor Hugo and Emile Zola. Since his death, his fiction has been translated into almost a hundred languages, and has formed the basis for more than 200 motion pictures.

THE MAN IN THE IRON MASK
[An Essay]

For nearly one hundred years this curious problem has exercised the imagination of writers of fiction—and of drama, and the patience of the learned in history. No subject is more obscure and elusive, and none more attractive to the general mind. It is a legend to the meaning of which none can find the key and yet in which everyone believes. Involuntarily we feel pity at the thought of that long captivity surrounded by so many extraordinary precautions, and when we dwell on the mystery which enveloped the captive, that pity is not only deepened but a kind of terror takes possession of us. It is very likely that if the name of the hero of this gloomy tale had been known at the time, he would now be forgotten. To give him a name would be to relegate him at once to the ranks of those commonplace offenders who quickly exhaust our interest and our tears. But this being, cut off from the world without leaving any discoverable trace, and whose disappearance apparently caused no void—this captive, distinguished among captives by the unexampled nature of his punishment, a prison within a prison, as if the walls of a mere cell were not narrow enough, has come to typify for us the sum of all the human misery and suffering ever inflicted by unjust tyranny.

Who was the Man in the Mask? Was he rapt away into this silent seclusion from the luxury of a court, from the intrigues of diplomacy, from the scaffold of a traitor, from the clash of battle? What did he leave behind? Love, glory, or a throne? What did he regret when hope had fled? Did he pour forth imprecations and curses on his tortures and blaspheme against high Heaven, or did he with a sigh possess his soul in patience?

The blows of fortune are differently received according to the different characters of those on whom they fall; and each one of us who in imagination threads the subterranean passages leading to the cells of Pignerol and Exilles, and incarcerates himself in the Iles Sainte-Marguerite and in the Bastille, the successive scenes of that long-protracted agony will give the prisoner a form shaped by his own fancy and a grief proportioned to his own power of suffering. How we long to pierce the thoughts and feel the heart-beats and watch the trickling tears behind that machine-like exterior, that impassible mask! Our imagination is powerfully excited by the dumbness of that fate borne by one whose words never reached the outward air, whose thoughts could never be read on the hidden features; by the isolation of forty years secured by two-fold barriers of stone and iron, and she clothes the object of her contemplation in majestic splendour, connects the mystery which enveloped his existence with mighty interests, and persists in regarding the prisoner as sacrificed for the preservation of some dynastic secret involving the peace of the world and the stability of a throne.

And when we calmly reflect on the whole case, do we feel that our first impulsively adopted opinion was wrong? Do we regard our belief as a poetical illusion? I do not think so;

on the contrary, it seems to me that our good sense approves our fancy's flight. For what can be more natural than the conviction that the secret of the name, age, and features of the captive, which was so perseveringly kept through long years at the cost of so much care, was of vital importance to the Government? No ordinary human passion, such as anger, hate, or vengeance, has so dogged and enduring a character; we feel that the measures taken were not the expression of a love of cruelty, for even supposing that Louis XIV were the most cruel of princes, would he not have chosen one of the thousand methods of torture ready to his hand before inventing a new and strange one? Moreover, why did he voluntarily burden himself with the obligation of surrounding a prisoner with such numberless precautions and such sleepless vigilance? Must he not have feared that in spite of it all the walls behind which he concealed the dread mystery would one day let in the light? Was it not through his entire reign a source of unceasing anxiety? And yet he respected the life of the captive whom it was so difficult to hide, and the discovery of whose identity would have been so dangerous. It would have been so easy to bury the secret in an obscure grave, and yet the order was never given. Was this an expression of hate, anger, or any other passion? Certainly not; the conclusion we must come to in regard to the conduct of the king is that all the measures he took against the prisoner were dictated by purely political motives; that his conscience, while allowing him to do everything necessary to guard the secret, did not permit him to take the further step of putting an end to the days of an unfortunate man, who in all probability was guilty of no crime.

Courtiers are seldom obsequious to the enemies of their master, so that we may regard the respect and consideration shown to the Man in the Mask by the governor Saint-Mars, and the minister Louvois, as a testimony, not only to his high rank, but also to his innocence.

For my part, I make no pretensions to the erudition of the bookworm, and I cannot read the history of the Man in the Iron Mask without feeling my blood boil at the abominable abuse of power—the heinous crime of which he was the victim.

A few years ago, M. Fournier and I, thinking the subject suitable for representation on the stage, undertook to read, before dramatising it, all the different versions of the affair which had been published up to that time. Since our piece was successfully performed at the Odeon two other versions have appeared: one was in the form of a letter addressed to the Historical Institute by M. Billiard, who upheld the conclusions arrived at by Soulavie, on whose narrative our play was founded; the other was a work by the bibliophile Jacob, who followed a new system of inquiry, and whose book displayed the results of deep research and extensive reading. It did not, however, cause me to change my opinion. Even had it been published before I had written my drama, I should still have adhered to the idea as to the most probable solution of the problem which I had arrived at in 1831, not only because it was incontestably the most dramatic, but also because it is supported by those moral presumptions which have such weight with us when considering a dark and doubtful question like the one before us. It will, be objected, perhaps, that dramatic writers, in their love of the marvellous and the pathetic, neglect logic and strain after effect, their aim being to obtain the applause of the gallery rather than the approbation of the learned. But to this it may be replied that the learned on their part sacrifice a great deal to their love of dates, more or less exact; to their desire to elucidate some point which had hitherto been considered obscure, and which their explanations do not always clear up; to the temptation to display their proficiency in the ingenious art of manipulating facts and figures culled from a dozen musty volumes into one consistent whole.

Our interest in this strange case of imprisonment arises, not alone from its completeness and duration, but also from our uncertainty as to the motives from which it was inflicted. Where erudition alone cannot suffice; where bookworm after bookworm, disdaining the conjectures of his predecessors, comes forward with a new theory founded on some forgotten document he has hunted out, only to find himself in his turn pushed into oblivion by some follower in his track, we must turn for guidance to some other light than that of scholarship; especially if, on strict investigation, we find that not one learned solution rests on a sound basis of fact.

In the question before us, which, as we said before, is a double one, asking not only who was the Man in the Iron

Mask, but why he was relentlessly subjected to this torture till the moment of his death, what we need in order to restrain our fancy is mathematical demonstration, and not philosophical induction.

While I do not go so far as to assert positively that Abbe Soulavie has once for all lifted the veil which hid the truth, I am yet persuaded that no other system of research is superior to his, and that no other suggested solution has so many presumptions in its favour. I have not reached this firm conviction on account of the great and prolonged success of our drama, but because of the ease with which all the opinions adverse to those of the abbe may be annihilated by pitting them one against the other.

The qualities that make for success being quite different in a novel and in a drama, I could easily have founded a romance on the fictitious loves of Buckingham and the queen, or on a supposed secret marriage between her and Cardinal Mazarin, calling to my aid a work by Saint-Mihiel which the bibliophile declares he has never read, although it is assuredly neither rare nor difficult of access. I might also have merely expanded my drama, restoring to the personages therein their true names and relative positions, both of which the exigencies of the stage had sometimes obliged me to alter, and while allowing them to fill the same parts, making them act more in accordance with historical fact. No fable however far-fetched, no grouping of characters however improbable, can, however, destroy the interest which the innumerable writings about the Iron Mask excite, although no two agree in details, and although each author and each witness declares himself in possession of complete knowledge. No work, however mediocre, however worthless even, which has appeared on this subject has ever failed of success, not even, for example, the strange jumble of Chevalier de Mouhy, a kind of literary braggart, who was in the pay of Voltaire, and whose work was published anonymously in 1746 by Pierre de Hondt of The Hague. It is divided into six short parts, and bears the title, 'Le Masque de Fer, ou les Aventures admirables du Prre et du Fils'. An absurd romance by Regnault Warin, and one at least equally absurd by Madame Guenard, met with a like favourable reception. In writing for the theatre, an author must choose one view of a dramatic situation to the exclusion of all others, and in following out this central idea is obliged by the inexorable laws of logic to push aside everything that interferes with its development. A book, on the contrary, is written to be discussed; it brings under the notice of the reader all the evidence produced at a trial which has as yet not reached a definite conclusion, and which in the case before us will never reach it, unless, which is most improbable, some lucky chance should lead to some new discovery.

The first mention of the prisoner is to be found in the 'Memoires secrets pour servir a l'Histoire de Perse' in one 12mo volume, by an anonymous author, published by the 'Compagnie des Libraires Associes d'Amsterdam' in 1745.

"Not having any other purpose," says the author (page 20, 2nd edit.), "than to relate facts which are not known, or about which no one has written, or about which it is impossible to be silent, we refer at once to a fact which has hitherto almost escaped notice concerning Prince Giafer (Louis de Bourbon, Comte de Vermandois, son of Louis XIV and Mademoiselle de la Valliere), who was visited by Ali-Momajou (the Duc d'Orleans, the regent) in the fortress of Ispahan (the Bastille), in which he had been imprisoned for several years. This visit had probably no other motive than to make sure that this prince was really alive, he having been reputed dead of the plague for over thirty years, and his obsequies having been celebrated in presence of an entire army.

"Cha-Abas (Louis XIV) had a legitimate son, Sephi-Mirza (Louis, Dauphin of France), and a natural son, Giafer. These two princes, as dissimilar in character as in birth, were always rivals and always at enmity with each other. One day Giafer so far forgot himself as to strike Sephi-Mirza. Cha-Abas having heard of the insult offered to the heir to the throne, assembled his most trusted councillors, and laid the conduct of the culprit before them—conduct which, according to the law of the country, was punishable with death, an opinion in which they all agreed. One of the councillors, however, sympathising more than the others with the distress of Cha-Abas, suggested that Giafer should be sent to the army, which was then on the frontiers of Feidrun (Flanders), and that his death from plague should be given out a few days after his arrival. Then, while the whole army was celebrating his obsequies, he should be carried off by night, in the greatest secrecy, to the stronghold on the isle of

Ormus (Sainte-Marguerite), and there imprisoned for life.

"This course was adopted, and carried out by faithful and discreet agents. The prince, whose premature death was mourned by the army, being carried by unfrequented roads to the isle of Ormus, was placed in the custody of the commandant of the island, who, had received orders beforehand not to allow any person whatever to see the prisoner. A single servant who was in possession of the secret was killed by the escort on the journey, and his face so disfigured by dagger thrusts that he could not be recognised.

"The commandant treated his prisoner with the most profound respect; he waited on him at meals himself, taking the dishes from the cooks at the door of the apartment, none of whom ever looked on the face of Giafer. One day it occurred to the prince to scratch, his name on the back of a plate with his knife. One of the servants into whose hands the plate fell ran with it at once to the commandant, hoping he would be pleased and reward the bearer; but the unfortunate man was greatly mistaken, for he was at once made away with, that his knowledge of such an important secret might be buried with himself.

"Giafer remained several years in the castle Ormus, and was then transported to the fortress of Ispahan; the commandant of Ormus having received the governorship of Ispahan as a reward for faithful service.

"At Ispahan, as at Ormus, whenever it was necessary on account of illness or any other cause to allow anyone to approach the prince, he was always masked; and several trustworthy persons have asserted that they had seen the masked prisoner often, and had noticed that he used the familiar 'tu' when addressing the governor, while the latter showed his charge the greatest respect. As Giafer survived Cha-Abas and Sephi-Mirza by many years, it may be asked why he was never set at liberty; but it must be remembered it would have been impossible to restore a prince to his rank and dignities whose tomb actually existed, and of whose burial there were not only living witnesses but documentary proofs, the authenticity of which it would have been useless to deny, so firm was the belief, which has lasted down to the present day, that Giafer died of the plague in camp when with the army on the frontiers of Flanders. Ali-Homajou died shortly after the visit he paid to Giafer."

This version of the story, which is the original source of all the controversy on the subject, was at first generally received as true. On a critical examination it fitted in very well with certain events which took place in the reign of Louis XIV.

The Comte de Vermandois had in fact left the court for the camp very soon after his reappearance there, for he had been banished by the king from his presence some time before for having, in company with several young nobles, indulged in the most reprehensible excesses.

"The king," says Mademoiselle de Montpensier ('Memoires de Mademoiselle de Montpensier', vol. xliii. p. 474., of 'Memoires Relatifs d'Histoire de France', Second Series, published by Petitot), "had not been satisfied with his conduct and refused to see him. The young prince had caused his mother much sorrow, but had been so well lectured that it was believed that he had at last turned over a new leaf." He only remained four days at court, reached the camp before Courtrai early in November 1683, was taken ill on the evening of the 12th, and died on the 19th of the same month of a malignant fever. Mademoiselle de Montpensier says that the Comte de Vermandois "fell ill from drink."

There are, of course, objections of all kinds to this theory.

For if, during the four days the comte was at court, he had struck the dauphin, everyone would have heard of the monstrous crime, and yet it is nowhere spoken of, except in the 'Memoires de Perse'. What renders the story of the blow still more improbable is the difference in age between the two princes. The dauphin, who already had a son, the Duc de Bourgogne, more than a year old, was born the 1st November 1661, and was therefore six years older than the Comte de Vermandois. But the most complete answer to the tale is to be found in a letter written by Barbezieux to Saint-Mars, dated the 13th August 1691:—

"When you have any information to send me relative to the prisoner who has been in your charge for twenty years, I most earnestly enjoin on you to take the same precautions as when you write to M. de Louvois."

The Comte de Vermandois, the official registration of whose death bears the date 1685, cannot have been twenty years a prisoner in 1691.

Six years after the Man in the Mask had been thus delivered over to the curiosity of the public, the 'Siecle de

Louis XIV' (2 vols. octavo, Berlin, 1751) was published by Voltaire under the pseudonym of M. de Francheville. Everyone turned to this work, which had been long expected, for details relating to the mysterious prisoner about whom everyone was talking.

Voltaire ventured at length to speak more openly of the prisoner than anyone had hitherto done, and to treat as a matter of history "an event long ignored by all historians." (vol. ii. p. 11, 1st edition, chap. xxv.). He assigned an approximate date to the beginning of this captivity, "some months after the death of Cardinal Mazarin" (1661); he gave a description of the prisoner, who according to him was "young and dark-complexioned; his figure was above the middle height and well proportioned; his features were exceedingly handsome, and his bearing was noble. When he spoke his voice inspired interest; he never complained of his lot, and gave no hint as to his rank." Nor was the mask forgotten: "The part which covered the chin was furnished with steel springs, which allowed the prisoner to eat without uncovering his face." And, lastly, he fixed the date of the death of the nameless captive; who "was buried," he says, "in 1704., by night, in the parish church of Saint-Paul."

Voltaire's narrative coincided with the account given in the 'Memoires de Peyse', save for the omission of the incident which, according to the 'Memoires', led in the first instance to the imprisonment of Giafer. "The prisoner," says Voltaire, "was sent to the Iles Sainte-Marguerite, and afterwards to the Bastille, in charge of a trusty official; he wore his mask on the journey, and his escort had orders to shoot him if he took it off. The Marquis de Louvois visited him while he was on the islands, and when speaking to him stood all the time in a respectful attitude. The prisoner was removed to the Bastille in 1690, where he was lodged as comfortably as could be managed in that building; he was supplied with everything he asked for, especially with the finest linen and the costliest lace, in both of which his taste was perfect; he had a guitar to play on, his table was excellent, and the governor rarely sat in his presence."

Voltaire added a few further details which had been given him by M. de Bernaville, the successor of M. de Saint-Mars, and by an old physician of the Bastille who had attended the prisoner whenever his health required a doctor, but who had never seen his face, although he had "often seen his tongue and his body." He also asserted that M. de Chamillart was the last minister who was in the secret, and that when his son-in-law, Marshal de la Feuillade, besought him on his knees, de Chamillart being on his deathbed, to tell him the name of the Man in the Iron Mask, the minister replied that he was under a solemn oath never to reveal the secret, it being an affair of state. To all these details, which the marshal acknowledges to be correct, Voltaire adds a remarkable note: "What increases our wonder is, that when the unknown captive was sent to the Iles Sainte-Marguerite no personage of note disappeared from the European stage."

The story of the Comte de Vermandois and the blow was treated as an absurd and romantic invention, which does not even attempt to keep within the bounds of the possible, by Baron C. (according to P. Marchand, Baron Crunyngen) in a letter inserted in the 'Bibliotheque raisonnee des Ouvrages des Savants de d'Europe', June 1745. The discussion was revived somewhat later, however, and a few Dutch scholars were supposed to be responsible for a new theory founded on history; the foundations proving somewhat shaky, however,—a quality which it shares, we must say, with all the other theories which have ever been advanced.

According to this new theory, the masked prisoner was a young foreign nobleman, groom of the chambers to Anne of Austria, and the real father of Louis XIV. This anecdote appears first in a duodecimo volume printed by Pierre Marteau at Cologne in 1692, and which bears the title, 'The Loves of Anne of Austria, Consort of Louis XIII, with M. le C. D. R., the Real Father of Louis XIV, King of France; being a Minute Account of the Measures taken to give an Heir to the Throne of France, the Influences at Work to bring this to pass, and the Denoument of the Comedy'.

This libel ran through five editions, bearing date successively, 1692, 1693, 1696, 1722, and 1738. In the title of the edition of 1696 the words "Cardinal de Richelieu" are inserted in place of the initials "C. D. R.," but that this is only a printer's error everyone who reads the work will perceive. Some have thought the three letters stood for Comte de Riviere, others for Comte de Rochefort, whose 'Memoires' compiled by Sandras de Courtilz supply these initials. The author of the book was an Orange writer in the pay of William

III, and its object was, he says, "to unveil the great mystery of iniquity which hid the true origin of Louis XIV." He goes on to remark that "the knowledge of this fraud, although comparatively rare outside France, was widely spread within her borders. The well-known coldness of Louis XIII; the extraordinary birth of Louis-Dieudonne, so called because he was born in the twenty-third year of a childless marriage, and several other remarkable circumstances connected with the birth, all point clearly to a father other than the prince, who with great effrontery is passed off by his adherents as such. The famous barricades of Paris, and the organised revolt led by distinguished men against Louis XIV on his accession to the throne, proclaimed aloud the king's illegitimacy, so that it rang through the country; and as the accusation had reason on its side, hardly anyone doubted its truth."

We give below a short abstract of the narrative, the plot of which is rather skilfully constructed:—

"Cardinal Richelieu, looking with satisfied pride at the love of Gaston, Duc d'Orleans, brother of the king, for his niece Parisiatis (Madame de Combalet), formed the plan of uniting the young couple in marriage. Gaston taking the suggestion as an insult, struck the cardinal. Pere Joseph then tried to gain the cardinal's consent and that of his niece to an attempt to deprive Gaston of the throne, which the childless marriage of Louis XIII seemed to assure him. A young man, the C. D. R. of the book, was introduced into Anne of Austria's room, who though a wife in name had long been a widow in reality. She defended herself but feebly, and on seeing the cardinal next day said to him, 'Well, you have had your wicked will; but take good care, sir cardinal, that I may find above the mercy and goodness which you have tried by many pious sophistries to convince me is awaiting me. Watch over my soul, I charge you, for I have yielded!' The queen having given herself up to love for some time, the joyful news that she would soon become a mother began to spread over the kingdom. In this manner was born Louis XIV, the putative son of Louis XIII. If this instalment of the tale be favourably received, says the pamphleteer, the sequel will soon follow, in which the sad fate of C. D. R. will be related, who was made to pay dearly for his short-lived pleasure."

Although the first part was a great success, the promised sequel never appeared. It must be admitted that such a story, though it never convinced a single person of the illegitimacy of Louis XIV, was an excellent prologue to the tale of the unfortunate lot of the Man in the Iron Mask, and increased the interest and curiosity with which that singular historical mystery was regarded. But the views of the Dutch scholars thus set forth met with little credence, and were soon forgotten in a new solution.

The third historian to write about the prisoner of the Iles Sainte-Marguerite was Lagrange-Chancel. He was just twenty-nine years of age when, excited by Freron's hatred of Voltaire, he addressed a letter from his country place, Antoniat, in Perigord, to the 'Annee Litteraire' (vol. iii. p. 188), demolishing the theory advanced in the 'Siecle de Louis XIV', and giving facts which he had collected whilst himself imprisoned in the same place as the unknown prisoner twenty years later.

"My detention in the Iles-Saint-Marguerite," says Lagrange-Chancel," brought many things to my knowledge which a more painstaking historian than M. de Voltaire would have taken the trouble to find out; for at the time when I was taken to the islands the imprisonment of the Man in the Iron Mask was no longer regarded as a state secret. This extraordinary event, which M. de Voltaire places in 1662, a few months after the death of Cardinal Mazarin, did not take place till 1669, eight years after the death of His Eminence. M. de La Motte-Guerin, commandant of the islands in my time, assured me that the prisoner was the Duc de Beaufort, who was reported killed at the siege of Candia, but whose body had never been recovered, as all the narratives of that event agree in stating. He also told me that M. de Saint-Mars, who succeeded Pignerol as governor of the islands, showed great consideration for the prisoner, that he waited on him at table, that the service was of silver, and that the clothes supplied to the prisoner were as costly as he desired; that when he was ill and in need of a physician or surgeon, he was obliged under pain of death to wear his mask in their presence, but that when he was alone he was permitted to pull out the hairs of his beard with steel tweezers, which were kept bright and polished. I saw a pair of these which had been actually used for this purpose in the possession of M. de Formanoir, nephew of Saint-Mars, and lieutenant of a Free Company raised for the purpose of guarding the prisoners. Several persons told me that when Saint-Mars, who had been placed over the Bastille, conducted his charge thither, the latter was heard to say behind his iron mask, 'Has the king designs on my life?' To which Saint-Mars replied, 'No, my prince; your life is safe: you must only let yourself be guided.'

"I also learned from a man called Dubuisson, cashier to the well-known Samuel Bernard, who, having been imprisoned for some years in the Bastile, was removed to the Iles Sainte-Marguerite, where he was confined along with some others in a room exactly over the one occupied by the unknown prisoner. He told me that they were able to communicate with him by means of the flue of the chimney, but on asking him why he persisted in not revealing his name and the cause of his imprisonment, he replied that such an avowal would be fatal not only to him but to those to whom he made it.

"Whether it were so or not, to-day the name and rank of this political victim are secrets the preservation of which is no longer necessary to the State; and I have thought that to tell the public what I know would cut short the long chain of circumstances which everyone was forging according to his fancy, instigated thereto by an author whose gift of relating the most impossible events in such a manner as to make them seem true has won for all his writings such success—even for his Vie de Charles XII"

This theory, according to Jacob, is more probable than

any of the others.

"Beginning with the year 1664.," he says, "the Duc de Beaufort had by his insubordination and levity endangered the success of several maritime expeditions. In October 1666 Louis XIV remonstrated with him with much tact, begging him to try to make himself more and more capable in the service of his king by cultivating the talents with which he was endowed, and ridding himself of the faults which spoilt his conduct. 'I do not doubt,' he concludes, 'that you will be all the more grateful to me for this mark of my benevolence towards you, when you reflect how few kings have ever shown their goodwill in a similar manner.'" ('Oeuvres de Louis XIV', vol. v. p. 388). Several calamities in the royal navy are known to have been brought about by the Duc de Beaufort. M. Eugene Sue, in his 'Histoire de la Marine', which is full of new and curious information, has drawn a very good picture of the position of the "roi des halles," the "king of the markets," in regard to Colbert and Louis XIV. Colbert wished to direct all the manoeuvres of the fleet from his study, while it was commanded by the naval grandmaster in the capricious manner which might be expected from his factious character and love of bluster (Eugene Sue, vol. i., 'Pieces Justificatives'). In 1699 Louis XIV sent the Duc de Beaufort to the relief of Candia, which the Turks were besieging. Seven hours after his arrival Beaufort was killed in a sortie. The Duc de Navailles, who shared with him the command of the French squadron, simply reported his death as follows: "He met a body of Turks who were pressing our troops hard: placing himself at the head of the latter, he fought valiantly, but at length his soldiers abandoned him, and we have not been able to learn his fate" ('Memoires du Duc de Navailles', book iv. P. 243)

The report of his death spread rapidly through France and Italy; magnificent funeral services were held in Paris, Rome, and Venice, and funeral orations delivered. Nevertheless, many believed that he would one day reappear, as his body had never been recovered.

Guy Patin mentions this belief, which he did not share, in two of his letters:—

"Several wagers have been laid that M. de Beaufort is not dead! 'O utinam'!" (Guy Patin, September 26, 1669).

"It is said that M. de Vivonne has been granted by commission the post of vice-admiral of France for twenty years; but there are many who believe that the Duc de Beaufort is not dead, but imprisoned in some Turkish island. Believe this who may, I don't; he is really dead, and the last thing I should desire would be to be as dead as he",(Ibid., January 14, 1670).

The following are the objections to this theory:

"In several narratives written by eye-witnesses of the siege of Candia," says Jacob, "it is related that the Turks, according to their custom, despoiled the body and cut off the head of the Duc de Beaufort on the field of battle, and that the latter was afterwards exhibited at Constantinople; and this may account for some of the details given by Sandras de Courtilz in his 'Memoires du Marquis de Montbrun' and his

'Memoires d'Artagnan', for one can easily imagine that the naked, headless body might escape recognition. M. Eugene Sue, in his 'Histoire de la Marine' (vol. ii, chap. 6), had adopted this view, which coincides with the accounts left by Philibert de Jarry and the Marquis de Ville, the MSS. of whose letters and 'Memoires' are to be found in the Bibliotheque du Roi.

"In the first volume of the 'Histoire de la Detention des Philosophes et des Gens de Lettres a la Bastille, etc.', we find the following passage:—

"Without dwelling on the difficulty and danger of an abduction, which an Ottoman scimitar might any day during this memorable siege render unnecessary, we shall restrict ourselves to declaring positively that the correspondence of Saint-Mars from 1669 to 1680 gives us no ground for supposing that the governor of Pignerol had any great prisoner of state in his charge during that period of time, except Fouquet and Lauzun.'"

While we profess no blind faith in the conclusions arrived at by the learned critic, we would yet add to the considerations on which he relies another, viz. that it is most improbable that Louis XIV should ever have considered it necessary to take such rigorous measures against the Duc de Beaufort. Truculent and self-confident as he was, he never acted against the royal authority in such a manner as to oblige the king to strike him down in secret; and it is difficult to believe that Louis XIV, peaceably seated on his throne, with all the enemies of his minority under his feet, should have revenged himself on the duke as an old Frondeur.

The critic calls our attention to another fact also adverse to the theory under consideration. The Man in the Iron Mask loved fine linen and rich lace, he was reserved in character and possessed of extreme refinement, and none of this suits the portraits of the 'roi des halles' which contemporary historians have drawn.

Regarding the anagram of the name Marchiali (the name under which the death of the prisoner was registered), 'hic amiral', as a proof, we cannot think that the gaolers of Pignerol amused themselves in propounding conundrums to exercise the keen intellect of their contemporaries; and moreover the same anagram would apply equally well to the Count of Vermandois, who was made admiral when only twenty-two months old. Abbe Papon, in his roamings through Provence, paid a visit to the prison in which the Iron Mask was confined, and thus speaks:—

"It was to the Iles Sainte-Marguerite that the famous prisoner with the iron mask whose name has never been discovered, was transported at the end of the last century; very few of those attached to his service were allowed to speak to him. One day, as M. de Saint-Mars was conversing with him, standing outside his door, in a kind of corridor, so as to be able to see from a distance everyone who approached, the son of one of the governor's friends, hearing the voices, came up; Saint-Mars quickly closed the door of the room, and, rushing to meet the young man, asked him with an air of great anxiety if he had overheard anything that was said. Having convinced himself that he had heard nothing, the

The Man In The Iron Mask [An Essay]

governor sent the young man away the same day, and wrote to the father that the adventure was like to have cost the son dear, and that he had sent him back to his home to prevent any further imprudence.

"I was curious enough to visit the room in which the unfortunate man was imprisoned, on the 2nd of February 1778. It is lighted by one window to the north, overlooking the sea, about fifteen feet above the terrace where the sentries paced to and fro. This window was pierced through a very thick wall and the embrasure barricaded by three iron bars, thus separating the prisoner from the sentries by a distance of over two fathoms. I found an officer of the Free Company in the fortress who was nigh on fourscore years old; he told me that his father, who had belonged to the same Company, had often related to him how a friar had seen something white floating on the water under the prisoner's window. On being fished out and carried to M. de Saint-Mars, it proved to be a shirt of very fine material, loosely folded together, and covered with writing from end to end. M. de Saint-Mars spread it out and read a few words, then turning to the friar who had brought it he asked him in an embarrassed manner if he had been led by curiosity to read any of the, writing. The friar protested repeatedly that he had not read a line, but nevertheless he was found dead in bed two days later. This incident was told so often to my informant by his father and by the chaplain of the fort of that time that he regarded it as incontestably true. The following fact also appears to me to be equally well established by the testimony of many witnesses.

I collected all the evidence I could on the spot, and also in the Lerins monastery, where the tradition is preserved.

"A female attendant being wanted for the prisoner, a woman of the village of Mongin offered herself for the place, being under the impression that she would thus be able to make her children's fortune; but on being told that she would not only never be allowed to see her children again, but would be cut off from the rest of the world as well, she refused to be shut up with a prisoner whom it cost so much to serve. I may mention here that at the two outer angles of the wall of the fort which faced the sea two sentries were placed, with orders to fire on any boat which approached within a certain distance.

"The prisoner's personal attendant died in the Iles Sainte-Marguerite. The brother of the officer whom I mentioned above was partly in the confidence of M. de Saint-Mars, and he often told how he was summoned to the prison once at midnight and ordered to remove a corpse, and that he carried it on his shoulders to the burial-place, feeling certain it was the prisoner who was dead; but it was only his servant, and it was then that an effort was made to supply his place by a female attendant."

Abbe Papon gives some curious details, hitherto unknown to the public, but as he mentions no names his narrative cannot be considered as evidence. Voltaire never replied to Lagrange-Chancel, who died the same year in which his letter was published. Freron desiring to revenge himself for the scathing portrait which Voltaire had drawn of him in the 'Ecossaise', called to his assistance a more redoubtable adversary than Lagrange-Chancel. Sainte-Foix had brought to the front a brand new theory, founded on a passage by Hume in an article in the 'Annee Litteraire (1768, vol. iv.), in which he maintained that the Man in the Iron Mask was the Duke of Monmouth, a natural son of Charles II, who was found guilty of high treason and beheaded in London on the 15th July 1685.

This is what the English historian says:

"It was commonly reported in London that the Duke of Monmouth's life had been saved, one of his adherents who bore a striking resemblance to the duke having consented to die in his stead, while the real culprit was secretly carried off to France, there to undergo a lifelong imprisonment."

The great affection which the English felt for the Duke of Monmouth, and his own conviction that the people only needed a leader to induce them to shake off the yoke of James II, led him to undertake an enterprise which might possibly have succeeded had it been carried out with prudence. He landed at Lyme, in Dorset, with only one hundred and twenty men; six thousand soon gathered round his standard; a few towns declared in his favour; he caused himself to be proclaimed king, affirming that he was born in wedlock, and that he possessed the proofs of the secret marriage of Charles II and Lucy Waiters, his mother. He met the Royalists on the battlefield, and victory seemed to be on his side, when just at the decisive moment his ammunition ran short. Lord Gray, who commanded the cavalry, beat a cowardly retreat, the unfortunate Monmouth was taken prisoner, brought to London, and beheaded.

The details published in the 'Siecle de Louis XIV' as to the personal appearance of the masked prisoner might have been taken as a description of Monmouth, who possessed great physical beauty. Sainte-Foix had collected every scrap of evidence in favour of his solution of the mystery, making use even of the following passage from an anonymous romance called 'The Loves of Charles II and James II, Kings of England':—

"The night of the pretended execution of the Duke of Monmouth, the king, attended by three men, came to the Tower and summoned the duke to his presence. A kind of loose cowl was thrown over his head, and he was put into a carriage, into which the king and his attendants also got, and was driven away."

Sainte-Foix also referred to the alleged visit of Saunders, confessor to James II, paid to the Duchess of Portsmouth after the death of that monarch, when the duchess took occasion to say that she could never forgive King James for consenting to Monmouth's execution, in spite of the oath he had taken on the sacred elements at the deathbed of Charles II that he would never take his natural brother's life, even in case of rebellion. To this the priest replied quickly, "The king kept his oath."

Hume also records this solemn oath, but we cannot say that all the historians agree on this point. 'The Universal History' by Guthrie and Gray, and the 'Histoire d'Angleterre'

The Man In The Iron Mask [An Essay]

by Rapin, Thoyras and de Barrow, do not mention it.

"Further," wrote Sainte-Foix, "an English surgeon called Nelaton, who frequented the Cafe Procope, much affected by men of letters, often related that during the time he was senior apprentice to a surgeon who lived near the Porte Saint-Antoine, he was once taken to the Bastille to bleed a prisoner. He was conducted to this prisoner's room by the governor himself, and found the patient suffering from violent headache. He spoke with an English accent, wore a gold-flowered dressing-gown of black and orange, and had his face covered by a napkin knotted behind his head."

This story does not hold water: it would be difficult to form a mask out of a napkin; the Bastille had a resident surgeon of its own as well as a physician and apothecary; no one could gain access to a prisoner without a written order from a minister, even the Viaticum could only be introduced by the express permission of the lieutenant of police.

This theory met at first with no objections, and seemed to be going to oust all the others, thanks, perhaps, to the combative and restive character of its promulgator, who bore criticism badly, and whom no one cared to incense, his sword being even more redoubtable than his pen.

It was known that when Saint-Mars journeyed with his prisoner to the Bastille, they had put up on the way at Palteau, in Champagne, a property belonging to the governor. Freron therefore addressed himself to a grand-nephew of Saint-Mars, who had inherited this estate, asking if he could give him any information about this visit. The following reply appeared in the 'Annee Litteraire (June 1768):—

"As it appears from the letter of M. de Sainte-Foix from which you quote that the Man in the Iron Mask still exercises the fancy of your journalists, I am willing to tell you all I know about the prisoner. He was known in the islands of Sainte-Marguerite and at the Bastille as 'La Tour.' The governor and all the other officials showed him great respect, and supplied him with everything he asked for that could be granted to a prisoner. He often took exercise in the yard of the prison, but never without his mask on. It was not till the 'Siecle' of M. de Voltaire appeared that I learned that the mask was of iron and furnished with springs; it may be that the circumstance was overlooked, but he never wore it except when taking the air, or when he had to appear before a stranger.

"M. de Blainvilliers, an infantry officer who was acquainted with M. de Saint-Mars both at Pignerol and Sainte-Marguerite, has often told me that the lot of 'La Tour' greatly excited his curiosity, and that he had once borrowed the clothes and arms of a soldier whose turn it was to be sentry on the terrace under the prisoner's window at Sainte-Marguerite, and undertaken the duty himself; that he had seen the prisoner distinctly, without his mask; that his face was white, that he was tall and well proportioned, except that his ankles were too thick, and that his hair was white, although he appeared to be still in the prime of life. He passed the whole of the night in question pacing to and fro in his room. Blainvilliers added that he was always dressed in brown, that he had plenty of fine linen and books, that the governor and the other officers always stood uncovered in his presence till he gave them leave to cover and sit down, and that they often bore him company at table.

"In 1698 M. de Saint-Mars was promoted from the governorship of the Iles Sainte-Marguerite to that of the Bastille. In moving thither, accompanied by his prisoner, he made his estate of Palteau a halting-place. The masked man arrived in a litter which preceded that of M. de Saint-Mars, and several mounted men rode beside it. The peasants were assembled to greet their liege lord. M. de Saint-Mars dined with his prisoner, who sat with his back to the dining-room windows, which looked out on the court. None of the peasants whom I have questioned were able to see whether the man kept his mask on while eating, but they all noticed that M. de Saint-Mars, who sat opposite to his charge, laid two pistols beside his plate; that only one footman waited at table, who went into the antechamber to change the plates and dishes, always carefully closing the dining-room door behind him. When the prisoner crossed the courtyard his face was covered with a black mask, but the peasants could see his lips and teeth, and remarked that he was tall, and had white hair. M. de Saint-Mars slept in a bed placed beside the prisoner's. M. de Blainvilliers told me also that 'as soon as he was dead, which happened in 1704, he was buried at Saint-Paul's,' and that 'the coffin was filled with substances which would rapidly consume the body.' He added, 'I never heard that the masked man spoke with an English accent.'"

Sainte-Foix proved the story related by M. de Blainvilliers to be little worthy of belief, showing by a circumstance mentioned in the letter that the imprisoned man could not be the Duc de Beaufort; witness the epigram of Madame de Choisy, "M. de Beaufort longs to bite and can't," whereas the peasants had seen the prisoner's teeth through his mask. It appeared as if the theory of Sainte-Foix were going to stand, when a Jesuit father, named Griffet, who was confessor at the Bastille, devoted chapter xiii, of his 'Traite des differentes Sortes de Preuves qui servent a etablir la Verite dans l'Histoire' (12mo, Liege, 1769) to the consideration of the Iron Mask. He was the first to quote an authentic document which certifies that the Man in the Iron Mask about whom there was so much disputing really existed. This was the written journal of M. du Jonca, King's Lieutenant in the Bastille in 1698, from which Pere Griffet took the following passage:—

"On Thursday, September the 8th, 1698, at three o'clock in the afternoon, M. de Saint-Mars, the new governor of the Bastille, entered upon his duties. He arrived from the islands of Sainte-Marguerite, bringing with him in a litter a prisoner whose name is a secret, and whom he had had under his charge there, and at Pignerol. This prisoner, who was always masked, was at first placed in the Bassiniere tower, where he remained until the evening. At nine o'clock p.m. I took him to the third room of the Bertaudiere tower, which I had had already furnished before his arrival with all needful articles, having received orders to do so from M. de Saint-Mars. While I was showing him the way to his room,

I was accompanied by M. Rosarges, who had also arrived along with M. de Saint-Mars, and whose office it was to wait on the said prisoner, whose table is to be supplied by the governor."

Du Jonca's diary records the death of the prisoner in the following terms:—

"Monday, 19th November 1703. The unknown prisoner, who always wore a black velvet mask, and whom M. de Saint-Mars brought with him from the Iles Sainte-Marguerite, and whom he had so long in charge, felt slightly unwell yesterday on coming back from mass. He died to-day at 10 p.m. without having a serious illness, indeed it could not have been slighter. M. Guiraut, our chaplain, confessed him yesterday, but as his death was quite unexpected he did not receive the last sacraments, although the chaplain was able to exhort him up to the moment of his death. He was buried on Tuesday the 20th November at 4 P.M. in the burial-ground of St. Paul's, our parish church. The funeral expenses amounted to 40 livres."

His name and age were withheld from the priests of the parish. The entry made in the parish register, which Pere Griffet also gives, is in the following words:—

"On the 19th November 1703, Marchiali, aged about forty-five, died in the Bastille, whose body was buried in the graveyard of Saint-Paul's, his parish, on the 20th instant, in the presence of M. Rosarges and of M. Reilh, Surgeon-Major of the Bastille.

"(Signed) ROSARGES.

"REILH."

As soon as he was dead everything belonging to him, without exception, was burned; such as his linen, clothes, bed and bedding, rugs, chairs, and even the doors of the room he occupied. His service of plate was melted down, the walls of his room were scoured and whitewashed, the very floor was renewed, from fear of his having hidden a note under it, or left some mark by which he could be recognised.

Pere Griffet did not agree with the opinions of either Lagrange-Chancel or Sainte-Foix, but seemed to incline towards the theory set forth in the 'Memoires de Perse', against which no irrefutable objections had been advanced. He concluded by saying that before arriving at any decision as to who the prisoner really was, it would be necessary to ascertain the exact date of his arrival at Pignerol.

Sainte-Foix hastened to reply, upholding the soundness of the views he had advanced. He procured from Arras a copy of an entry in the registers of the Cathedral Chapter, stating that Louis XIV had written with his own hand to the said Chapter that they were to admit to burial the body of the Comte de Vermandois, who had died in the city of Courtrai; that he desired that the deceased should be interred in the centre of the choir, in the vault in which lay the remains of Elisabeth, Comtesse de Vermandois, wife of Philip of Alsace, Comte de Flanders, who had died in 1182. It is not to be supposed that Louis XIV would have chosen a family vault in which to bury a log of wood.

Sainte-Foix was, however, not acquainted with the letter

of Barbezieux, dated the 13th August 1691, to which we have already referred, as a proof that the prisoner was not the Comte de Vermandois; it is equally a proof that he was not the Duke of Monmouth, as Sainte-Foix maintained; for sentence was passed on the Duke of Monmouth in 1685, so that it could not be of him either that Barbezieux wrote in 1691, "The prisoner whom you have had in charge for twenty years."

In the very year in which Sainte-Foix began to flatter himself that his theory was successfully established, Baron Heiss brought a new one forward, in a letter dated "Phalsburg, 28th June 1770," and addressed to the 'Journal Enclycopedique'. It was accompanied by a letter translated from the Italian which appeared in the 'Histoire Abregee de l'Europe' by Jacques Bernard, published by Claude Jordan, Leyden, 1685-87, in detached sheets. This letter stated (August 1687, article 'Mantoue') that the Duke of Mantua being desirous to sell his capital, Casale, to the King of France, had been dissuaded therefrom by his secretary, and induced to join the other princes of Italy in their endeavours to thwart the ambitious schemes of Louis XVI. The Marquis d'Arcy, French ambassador to the court of Savoy, having been informed of the secretary's influence, distinguished him by all kinds of civilities, asked him frequently to table, and at last invited him to join a large hunting party two or three leagues outside Turin. They set out together, but at a short distance from the city were surrounded by a dozen horsemen, who carried off the secretary, 'disguised him, put a mask on him, and took him to Pignerol.' He was not kept long in this fortress, as it was 'too near the Italian frontier, and although he was carefully guarded it was feared that the walls would speak'; so he was transferred to the Iles Sainte-Marguerite, where he is at present in the custody of M. de Saint-Mars.

This theory, of which much was heard later, did not at first excite much attention. What is certain is that the Duke of Mantua's secretary, by name Matthioli, was arrested in 1679 through the agency of Abbe d'Estrade and M. de Catinat, and taken with the utmost secrecy to Pignerol, where he was imprisoned and placed in charge of M. de Saint-Mars. He must not, however, be confounded with the Man in the Iron Mask.

Catinat says of Matthioli in a letter to Louvois "No one knows the name of this knave."

Louvois writes to Saint-Mars: "I admire your patience in waiting for an order to treat such a rogue as he deserves, when he treats you with disrespect."

Saint-Mars replies to the minister: "I have charged Blainvilliers to show him a cudgel and tell him that with its aid we can make the froward meek."

Again Louvois writes: "The clothes of such people must be made to last three or four years."

This cannot have been the nameless prisoner who was treated with such consideration, before whom Louvois stood bare-headed, who was supplied with fine linen and lace, and so on.

Altogether, we gather from the correspondence of Saint-

Mars that the unhappy man alluded to above was confined along with a mad Jacobin, and at last became mad himself, and succumbed to his misery in 1686.

Voltaire, who was probably the first to supply such inexhaustible food for controversy, kept silence and took no part in the discussions. But when all the theories had been presented to the public, he set about refuting them. He made himself very merry, in the seventh edition of 'Questions sur l'Encyclopedie distibuees en forme de Dictionnaire (Geneva, 1791), over the complaisance attributed to Louis XIV in acting as police-sergeant and gaoler for James II, William III, and Anne, with all of whom he was at war. Persisting still in taking 1661 or 1662 as the date when the incarceration of the masked prisoner began, he attacks the opinions advanced by Lagrange-Chancel and Pere Griffet, which they had drawn from the anonymous 'Memoires secrets pour servir a l'Histoire de Perse'. "Having thus dissipated all these illusions," he says, "let us now consider who the masked prisoner was, and how old he was when he died. It is evident that if he was never allowed to walk in the courtyard of the Bastille or to see a physician without his mask, it must have been lest his too striking resemblance to someone should be remarked; he could show his tongue but not his face. As regards his age, he himself told the apothecary at the Bastille, a few days before his death, that he thought he was about sixty; this I have often heard from a son-in-law to this apothecary, M. Marsoban, surgeon to Marshal Richelieu, and afterwards to the regent, the Duc d'Orleans. The writer of this article knows perhaps more on this subject than Pere Griffet. But he has said his say."

This article in the 'Questions on the Encyclopaedia' was followed by some remarks from the pen of the publisher, which are also, however, attributed by the publishers of Kelh to Voltaire himself. The publisher, who sometimes calls himself the author, puts aside without refutation all the theories advanced, including that of Baron Heiss, and says he has come to the conclusion that the Iron Mask was, without doubt, a brother and an elder brother of Louis XIV, by a lover of the queen. Anne of Austria had come to persuade herself that hers alone was the fault which had deprived Louis XIII [the publisher of this edition overlooked the obvious typographical error of "XIV" here when he meant, and it only makes sense, that it was XIII. D.W.] of an heir, but the birth of the Iron Mask undeceived her. The cardinal, to whom she confided her secret, cleverly arranged to bring the king and queen, who had long lived apart, together again. A second son was the result of this reconciliation; and the first child being removed in secret, Louis XIV remained in ignorance of the existence of his half-brother till after his majority. It was the policy of Louis XIV to affect a great respect for the royal house, so he avoided much embarrassment to himself and a scandal affecting the memory of Anne of Austria by adopting the wise and just measure of burying alive the pledge of an adulterous love. He was thus enabled to avoid committing an act of cruelty, which a sovereign less conscientious and less magnanimous would have considered a necessity.

The Man In The Iron Mask [An Essay]

After this declaration Voltaire made no further reference to the Iron Mask. This last version of the story upset that of Sainte-Foix. Voltaire having been initiated into the state secret by the Marquis de Richelieu, we may be permitted to suspect that being naturally indiscreet he published the truth from behind the shelter of a pseudonym, or at least gave a version which approached the truth, but later on realising the dangerous significance of his words, he preserved for the future complete silence.

We now approach the question whether the prince who thus became the Iron Mask was an illegitimate brother or a twin-brother of Louis XIV. The first was maintained by M. Quentin-Crawfurd; the second by Abbe Soulavie in his 'Memoires du Marechal Duc de Richelieu' (London, 1790). In 1783 the Marquis de Luchet, in the 'Journal des Gens du Monde' (vol. iv. No. 23, p. 282, et seq.), awarded to Buckingham the honour of the paternity in dispute. In support of this, he quoted the testimony of a lady of the house of Saint-Quentin who had been a mistress of the minister Barbezieux, and who died at Chartres about the middle of the eighteenth century. She had declared publicly that Louis XIV had consigned his elder brother to perpetual imprisonment, and that the mask was necessitated by the close resemblance of the two brothers to each other.

The Duke of Buckingham, who came to France in 1625, in order to escort Henrietta Maria, sister of Louis XIII, to England, where she was to marry the Prince of Wales, made no secret of his ardent love for the queen, and it is almost certain that she was not insensible to his passion. An anonymous pamphlet, 'La Conference du Cardinal Mazarin avec le Gazetier' (Brussels, 1649), says that she was infatuated about him, and allowed him to visit her in her room. She even permitted him to take off and keep one of her gloves, and his vanity leading him to show his spoil, the king heard of it, and was vastly offended. An anecdote, the truth of which no one has ever denied, relates that one day Buckingham spoke to the queen with such passion in the presence of her lady-in-waiting, the Marquise de Senecey, that the latter exclaimed, "Be silent, sir, you cannot speak thus to the Queen of France!" According to this version, the Man in the Iron Mask must have been born at latest in 1637, but the mention of any such date would destroy the possibility of Buckingham's paternity; for he was assassinated at Portsmouth on September 2nd, 1628.

After the taking of the Bastille the masked prisoner became the fashionable topic of discussion, and one heard of nothing else. On the 13th of August 1789 it was announced in an article in a journal called 'Loisirs d'un Patriote francais', which was afterwards published anonymously as a pamphlet, that the publisher had seen, among other documents found in the Bastille, a card bearing the unintelligible number "64389000," and the following note: "Fouquet, arriving from Les Iles Sainte-Marguerite in an iron mask." To this there was, it was said, a double signature, viz. "XXX," superimposed on the name "Kersadion." The journalist was of opinion that Fouquet had succeeded in making his escape, but had been retaken and condemned to pass for dead, and to wear a mask henceforward, as a punishment for his attempted evasion. This tale made some impression, for it was remembered that in the Supplement to the 'Siecle de Louis XIV' it was stated that Chamillart had said that "the Iron Mask was a man who knew all the secrets of M. Fouquet." But the existence of this card was never proved, and we cannot accept the story on the unsupported word of an anonymous writer.

From the time that restrictions on the press were removed, hardly a day passed without the appearance of some new pamphlet on the Iron Mask. Louis Dutens, in 'Correspondence interceptee' (12mo, 1789), revived the theory of Baron Heiss, supporting it by new and curious facts. He proved that Louis XIV had really ordered one of the Duke of Mantua's ministers to be carried off and imprisoned in Pignerol. Dutens gave the name of the victim as Girolamo Magni. He also quoted from a memorandum which by the wish of the Marquis de Castellane was drawn up by a certain Souchon, probably the man whom Papon questioned in 1778. This Souchon was the son of a man who had belonged to the Free Company maintained in the islands in the time of Saint-Mars, and was seventy-nine years old. This memorandum gives a detailed account of the abduction of a minister in 1679, who is styled a "minister of the Empire," and his arrival as a masked prisoner at the islands, and states that he died there in captivity nine years after he was carried off.

Dutens thus divests the episode of the element of the

marvellous with which Voltaire had surrounded it. He called to his aid the testimony of the Duc de Choiseul, who, having in vain attempted to worm the secret of the Iron Mask out of Louis XV, begged Madame de Pompadour to try her hand, and was told by her that the prisoner was the minister of an Italian prince. At the same time that Dutens wrote, "There is no fact in history better established than the fact that the Man in the Iron Mask was a minister of the Duke of Mantua who was carried off from Turin," M. Quentin-Crawfurd was maintaining that the prisoner was a son of Anne of Austria; while a few years earlier Bouche, a lawyer, in his 'Essai sur l'Histoire de Provence' (2 vols. 4to, 1785), had regarded this story as a fable invented by Voltaire, and had convinced himself that the prisoner was a woman. As we see, discussion threw no light on the subject, and instead of being dissipated, the confusion became ever "worse confounded."

In 1790 the 'Memoires du Marechal de Richelieu' appeared. He had left his note-books, his library, and his correspondence to Soulavie. The 'Memoires' are undoubtedly authentic, and have, if not certainty, at least a strong moral presumption in their favour, and gained the belief of men holding diverse opinions. But before placing under the eyes of our readers extracts from them relating to the Iron Mask, let us refresh our memory by recalling two theories which had not stood the test of thorough investigation.

According to some MS. notes left by M. de Bonac, French ambassador at Constantinople in 1724, the Armenian Patriarch Arwedicks, a mortal enemy of our Church and the instigator of the terrible persecutions to which the Roman Catholics were subjected, was carried off into exile at the request of the Jesuits by a French vessel, and confined in a prison whence there was no escape. This prison was the fortress of Sainte-Marguerite, and from there he was taken to the Bastille, where he died. The Turkish Government continually clamoured for his release till 1723, but the French Government persistently denied having taken any part in the abduction.

Even if it were not a matter of history that Arwedicks went over to the Roman Catholic Church and died a free man in Paris, as may be seen by an inspection of the certificate of his death preserved among the archives in the Foreign Office, one sentence from the note-book of M. de Bonac would be sufficient to annihilate this theory. M. de Bonac says that the Patriarch was carried off, while M. de Feriol, who succeeded M. de Chateauneuf in 1699, was ambassador at Constantinople. Now it was in 1698 that Saint-Mars arrived at the Bastille with his masked prisoner.

Several English scholars have sided with Gibbon in thinking that the Man in the Iron Mask might possibly have been Henry, the second son of Oliver Cromwell, who was held as a hostage by Louis XIV.

By an odd coincidence the second son of the Lord Protector does entirely disappear from the page of history in 1659; we know nothing of where he afterwards lived nor when he died. But why should he be a prisoner of state in France, while his elder brother Richard was permitted to live there quite openly? In the absence of all proof, we cannot attach the least importance to this explanation of the mystery.

We now come to the promised extracts from the 'Memoires du Marechal de Richelieu':

"Under the late king there was a time when every class of society was asking who the famous personage really was who went by the name of the Iron Mask, but I noticed that this curiosity abated somewhat after his arrival at the Bastille with Saint-Mars, when it began to be reported that orders had been given to kill him should he let his name be known. Saint-Mars also let it be understood that whoever found out the secret would share the same fate. This threat to murder both the prisoner and those who showed too much curiosity about him made such an impression, that during the lifetime of the late king people only spoke of the mystery below their breath. The anonymous author of 'Les Memoires de Perse', which were published in Holland fifteen years after the death of Louis XIV, was the first who dared to speak publicly of the prisoner and relate some anecdotes about him.

"Since the publication of that work, liberty of speech and the freedom of the press have made great strides, and the shade of Louis XIV having lost its terrors, the case of the Iron Mask is freely discussed, and yet even now, at the end of my life and seventy years after the death of the king, people are still asking who the Man in the Iron Mask really was.

"This question was one I put to the adorable princess, beloved of the regent, who inspired in return only aversion and respect, all her love being given to me. As everyone was persuaded that the regent knew the name, the course of life, and the cause of the imprisonment of the masked prisoner, I, being more venturesome in my curiosity than others, tried through my princess to fathom the secret. She had hitherto constantly repulsed the advances of the Duc d' Orleans, but as the ardour of his passion was thereby in no wise abated, the least glimpse of hope would be sufficient to induce him to grant her everything she asked; I persuaded her, therefore, to let him understand that if he would allow her to read the 'Memoires du Masque' which were in his possession his dearest desires would be fulfilled.

"The Duc d'Orleans had never been known to reveal any secret of state, being unspeakably circumspect, and having been trained to keep every confidence inviolable by his preceptor Dubois, so I felt quite certain that even the princess would fail in her efforts to get a sight of the memoranda in his possession relative to the birth and rank of the masked prisoner; but what cannot love, and such an ardent love, induce a man to do?

"To reward her goodness the regent gave the documents into her hands, and she forwarded them to me next day, enclosed in a note written in cipher, which, according to the laws of historical writing, I reproduce in its entirety, vouching for its authenticity; for the princess always employed a cipher when she used the language of gallantry, and this note told me what treaty she had had to sign in order that she might obtain the documents, and the duke the desire of his heart. The details are not admissible in serious history, but, borrowing the modest language of the patriarchal time, I may say that if Jacob, before he obtained possession of the best beloved of Laban's daughters, was obliged to pay the price twice over, the regent drove a better bargain than the patriarch. The note and the memorandum were as follows:

"'2. 1. 17. 12. 9. 2. 20. 2. 1. 7. 14 20. 10. 3. 21. 1. 11. 14. 1. 15. 16. 12. 17. 14. 2. 1. 21. 11. 20. 17. 12. 9. 14. 9. 2. 8. 20. 5. 20. 2. 2. 17. 8. 1. 2. 20. 9. 21. 21. 1. 5. 12. 17. 15. 00. 14. 1. 15. 14. 12. 9. 21. 5. 12. 9. 21. 16. 20. 14. 8. 3.

"NARRATIVE OF THE BIRTH AND EDUCATION OF THE UNFORTUNATE PRINCE WHO WAS SEPARATED FROM THE WORLD BY CARDINALS RICHELIEU AND MAZARIN AND IMPRISONED BY ORDER OF LOUIS XIV.

"'Drawn up by the Governor of this Prince on his deathbed.

"'The unfortunate prince whom I brought up and had in charge till almost the end of my life was born on the 5th September 1638 at 8.30 o'clock in the evening, while the king was at supper. His brother, who is now on the throne, was born at noon while the king was at dinner, but whereas his birth was splendid and public, that of his brother was sad and secret; for the king being informed by the midwife that the queen was about to give birth to a second child, ordered the chancellor, the midwife, the chief almoner, the queen's confessor, and myself to stay in her room to be witnesses of whatever happened, and of his course of action should a second child be born.

"'For a long time already it had been foretold to the king that his wife would give birth to two sons, and some days before, certain shepherds had arrived in Paris, saying they were divinely inspired, so that it was said in Paris that if two dauphins were born it would be the greatest misfortune which could happen to the State. The Archbishop of Paris summoned these soothsayers before him, and ordered them to be imprisoned in Saint-Lazare, because the populace was becoming excited about them—a circumstance which filled the king with care, as he foresaw much trouble to his kingdom. What had been predicted by the soothsayers happened, whether they had really been warned by the constellations, or whether Providence by whom His Majesty had been warned of the calamities which might happen to France interposed. The king had sent a messenger to the cardinal to tell him of this prophecy, and the cardinal had replied that the matter, must be considered, that the birth of two dauphins was not impossible, and should such a case arrive, the second must be carefully hidden away, lest in the future desiring to be king he should fight against his brother in support of a new branch of the royal house, and come at last to reign.

"'The king in his suspense felt very uncomfortable, and as the queen began to utter cries we feared a second confinement. We sent to inform the king, who was almost overcome by the thought that he was about to become the father of two dauphins. He said to the Bishop of Meaux, whom he had sent for to minister to the queen, "Do not quit my wife till she is safe; I am in mortal terror." Immediately after he summoned us all, the Bishop of Meaux, the chancellor M. Honorat, Dame Peronete the midwife, and myself, and said to us in presence of the queen, so that she could hear, that we would answer to him with our heads if we made known the birth of a second dauphin; that it was his will that the fact should remain a state secret, to prevent the misfortunes which would else happen, the Salic Law not having declared to whom the inheritance of the kingdom should come in case two eldest sons were born to any of the kings.

"What had been foretold happened: the queen, while the king was at supper, gave birth to a second dauphin, more dainty and more beautiful than the first, but who wept and wailed unceasingly, as if he regretted to take up that life in which he was afterwards to endure such suffering. The chancellor drew up the report of this wonderful birth, without parallel in our history; but His Majesty not being pleased with its form, burned it in our presence, and the chancellor had to write and rewrite till His Majesty was satisfied. The almoner remonstrated, saying it would be impossible to hide the birth of a prince, but the king returned that he had reasons of state for all he did.

"Afterwards the king made us register our oath, the chancellor signing it first, then the queen's confessor, and I last. The oath was also signed by the surgeon and midwife who attended on the queen, and the king attached this document to the report, taking both away with him, and I never heard any more of either. I remember that His Majesty consulted with the chancellor as to the form of the oath, and that he spoke for a long time in an undertone to the cardinal: after which the last-born child was given into the charge of the midwife, and as they were always afraid she would babble about his birth, she has told me that they often threatened her with death should she ever mention it: we were also forbidden to speak, even to each other, of the child whose birth we had witnessed.

"'Not one of us has as yet violated his oath; for His Majesty dreaded nothing so much as a civil war brought about by the two children born together, and the cardinal, who afterwards got the care of the second child into his hands, kept that fear alive. The king also commanded us to examine the unfortunate prince minutely; he had a wart above the left elbow, a mole on the right side of his neck, and a tiny wart on his right thigh; for His Majesty was determined, and rightly so, that in case of the decease of the first-born, the royal infant whom he was entrusting to our care should take his place; wherefore he required our signmanual to the report of the birth, to which a small royal seal was attached in our presence, and we all signed it after His Majesty, according as he commanded. As to the shepherds who had foretold the double birth, never did I hear another word of them, but neither did I inquire. The cardinal who took the mysterious infant in charge probably got them out of the country.

"'All through the infancy of the second prince Dame Peronete treated him as if he were her own child, giving out that his father was a great nobleman; for everyone saw by the care she lavished on him and the expense she went to, that although unacknowledged he was the cherished son of rich parents, and well cared for.

"'When the prince began to grow up, Cardinal Mazarin, who succeeded Cardinal Richelieu in the charge of the prince's education, gave him into my hands to bring up in a manner worthy of a king's son, but in secret. Dame Peronete continued in his service till her death, and was very much attached to him, and he still more to her. The prince was instructed in my house in Burgundy, with all the care due to the son and brother of a king.

"'I had several conversations with the queen mother during the troubles in France, and Her Majesty always seemed to fear that if the existence of the prince should be discovered during the lifetime of his brother, the young king, malcontents would make it a pretext for rebellion, because many medical men hold that the last-born of twins is in reality the elder, and if so, he was king by right, while many others have a different opinion.

"'In spite of this dread, the queen could never bring herself to destroy the written evidence of his birth, because in case of the death of the young king she intended to have his twin-brother proclaimed. She told me often that the written proofs were in her strong box.

"'I gave the ill-starred prince such an education as I should have liked to receive myself, and no acknowledged son of a king ever had a better. The only thing for which I have to reproach myself is that, without intending it, I caused him great unhappiness; for when he was nineteen years old he had a burning desire to know who he was, and as he saw that I was determined to be silent, growing more firm the more he tormented me with questions, he made up his mind henceforward to disguise his curiosity and to make me think that he believed himself a love-child of my own. He began to call me 'father,' although when we were alone I often assured him that he was mistaken; but at length I gave up combating this belief, which he perhaps only feigned to make me speak, and allowed him to think he was my son, contradicting him no more; but while he continued to dwell on this subject he was meantime making every effort to find out who he really was. Two years passed thus, when, through an unfortunate piece of forgetfulness on my part, for which I greatly blame myself, he became acquainted with the truth. He knew that the king had lately sent me several messengers, and once having carelessly forgotten to lock up a casket containing letters from the queen and the cardinals, he read part and divined the rest through his natural intelligence; and later confessed to me that he had carried off the letter which told most explicitly of his birth.

"'I can recall that from this time on, his manner to me showed no longer that respect for me in which I had brought him up, but became hectoring and rude, and that I could not imagine the reason of the change, for I never found out that he had searched my papers, and he never revealed to me how he got at the casket, whether he was aided by some workmen whom he did not wish to betray, or had employed other means.

"'One day, however, he unguardedly asked me to show him the portraits of the late and the present king. I answered that those that existed were so poor that I was waiting till better ones were taken before having them in my house.

"'This answer, which did not satisfy him, called forth the request to be allowed to go to Dijon. I found out afterwards that he wanted to see a portrait of the king which was there, and to get to the court, which was just then at Saint-Jean-de-Luz, because of the approaching marriage with the infanta; so that he might compare himself with his brother and see if there were any resemblance between them. Having knowledge of his plan, I never let him out of my sight.

"'The young prince was at this time as beautiful as Cupid, and through the intervention of Cupid himself he succeeded in getting hold of a portrait of his brother. One of the upper servants of the house, a young girl, had taken his fancy, and he lavished such caresses on her and inspired her with so much love, that although the whole household was strictly forbidden to give him anything without my permission, she procured him a portrait of the king. The unhappy prince saw the likeness at once, indeed no one could help seeing it, for the one portrait would serve equally well for either brother, and the sight produced such a fit of fury that he came to me crying out, "There is my brother, and this tells me who I am!" holding out a letter from Cardinal Mazarin which he had stolen from me, and making a great commotion in my house.

"'The dread lest the prince should escape and succeed in appearing at the marriage of his brother made me so uneasy, that I sent off a messenger to the king to tell him that my casket had been opened, and asking for instructions. The king sent back word through the cardinal that we were both to be shut up till further orders, and that the prince was to be made to understand that the cause of our common misfortune was his absurd claim. I have since shared his prison, but I believe that a decree of release has arrived from my heavenly judge, and for my soul's health and for my ward's sake I make this declaration, that he may know what measures to take in order to put an end to his ignominious estate should the king die without children. Can any oath imposed under threats oblige one to be silent about such incredible events, which it is nevertheless necessary that posterity should know?'"

Such were the contents of the historical document given by the regent to the princess, and it suggests a crowd of questions. Who was the prince's governor? Was he a Burgundian? Was he simply a landed proprietor, with some property and a country house in Burgundy? How far was his estate from Dijon? He must have been a man of note, for he enjoyed the most intimate confidence at the court of Louis XIII, either by virtue of his office or because he was a favourite of the king, the queen, and Cardinal Richelieu. Can we learn from the list of the nobles of Burgundy what member of their body disappeared from public life along with a young ward whom he had brought up in his own house just after the marriage of Louis XIV? Why did he not attach his signature to the declaration, which appears to be a hundred years old? Did he dictate it when so near death that he had not strength to sign it? How did it find its way out of prison? And so forth.

There is no answer to all these questions, and I, for my part, cannot undertake to affirm that the document is genuine. Abbe Soulavie relates that he one day "pressed the marshal for an answer to some questions on the matter, asking, amongst other things, if it were not true that the prisoner was an elder brother of Louis XIV born without the knowledge of Louis XIII. The marshal appeared very much embarrassed, and although he did not entirely refuse to answer, what he said was not very explanatory. He averred that this important personage was neither the illegitimate brother of Louis XIV, nor the Duke of Monmouth, nor the Comte de Vermandois, nor the Duc de Beaufort, and so on, as so many writers had asserted." He called all their writings mere inventions, but added that almost every one of them had got hold of some true incidents, as for instance the order to kill the prisoner should he make himself known. Finally he acknowledged that he knew the state secret, and used the following words: "All that I can tell you, abbe, is, that when the prisoner died at the beginning of the century, at a very advanced age, he had ceased to be of such importance as when, at the beginning of his reign, Louis XIV shut him up for weighty reasons of state."

The above was written down under the eyes of the marshal, and when Abbe Soulavie entreated him to say something further which, while not actually revealing the secret, would yet satisfy his questioner's curiosity, the marshal answered, "Read M. de Voltaire's latest writings on the subject, especially his concluding words, and reflect on them."

With the exception of Dulaure, all the critics have treated Soulavie's narrative with the most profound contempt, and we must confess that if it was an invention it was a monstrous one, and that the concoction of the famous note in cipher was abominable. "Such was the great secret; in order to find it out, I had to allow myself 5, 12, 17, 15, 14, 1, three times by 8, 3." But unfortunately for those who would defend the morals of Mademoiselle de Valois, it would be difficult to traduce the character of herself, her lover, and her father, for what one knows of the trio justifies one in believing that the more infamous the conduct imputed to them, the more likely it is to be true. We cannot see the force of the objection that Louvois would not have written in the following terms to Saint-Mars in 1687 about a bastard son of Anne of Austria: "I see no objection to your removing Chevalier de Thezut from the prison in which he is confined, and putting your prisoner there till the one you are preparing for him is ready to receive him." And we cannot understand those who ask if Saint-Mars, following the example of the minister, would have said of a prince "Until he is installed in the prison which is being prepared for him here, which has a chapel adjoining"? Why should he have expressed himself otherwise? Does it evidence an abatement of consideration to call a prisoner a prisoner, and his prison a prison?

A certain M. de Saint-Mihiel published an 8vo volume

in 1791, at Strasbourg and Paris, entitled 'Le veritable homme, dit au MASQUE DE FER, ouvrage dans lequel on fait connaitre, sur preuves incontestables, a qui le celebre infortune dut le jour, quand et ou il naquit'. The wording of the title will give an idea of the bizarre and barbarous jargon in which the whole book is written. It would be difficult to imagine the vanity and self-satisfaction which inspire this new reader of riddles. If he had found the philosopher's stone, or made a discovery which would transform the world, he could not exhibit more pride and pleasure. All things considered, the "incontestable proofs" of his theory do not decide the question definitely, or place it above all attempts at refutation, any more than does the evidence on which the other theories which preceded and followed his rest. But what he lacks before all other things is the talent for arranging and using his materials. With the most ordinary skill he might have evolved a theory which would have defied criticism at least as successfully, as the others, and he might have supported it by proofs, which if not incontestable (for no one has produced such), had at least moral presumption in their favour, which has great weight in such a mysterious and obscure affair, in trying to explain, which one can never leave on one side, the respect shown by Louvois to the prisoner, to whom he always spoke standing and with uncovered head.

According to M. de Saint-Mihiel, the 'Man in the Iron Mask was a legitimate son of Anne of Austria and Mazarin'.

He avers that Mazarin was only a deacon, and not a priest, when he became cardinal, having never taken priest's orders, according to the testimony of the Princess Palatine, consort of Philip I, Duc d'Orleans, and that it was therefore possible for him to marry, and that he did marry, Anne of Austria in secret.

"Old Madame Beauvais, principal woman of the bed-chamber to the queen mother, knew of this ridiculous marriage, and as the price of her secrecy obliged the queen to comply with all her whims. To this circumstance the principal bed-chamber women owe the extensive privileges accorded them ever since in this country" (Letter of the Duchesse d'Orleans, 13th September 1713).

"The queen mother, consort of Louis XIII, had done worse than simply to fall in love with Mazarin, she had married him, for he had never been an ordained priest, he had only taken deacon's orders. If he had been a priest his marriage would have been impossible. He grew terribly tired of the good queen mother, and did not live happily with her, which was only what he deserved for making such a marriage" (Letter of the Duchesse d'Orleans, 2nd November 1717).

"She (the queen mother) was quite easy in her conscience about Cardinal Mazarin; he was not in priest's orders, and so could marry. The secret passage by which he reached the queen's rooms every evening still exists in the Palais Royal" (Letter of the Duchesse d'Orleans, 2nd July 1719)

"The queen's, manner of conducting affairs is influenced by the passion which dominates her. When she and the cardinal converse together, their ardent love for each other is betrayed by their looks and gestures; it is plain to see that when obliged to part for a time they do it with great reluctance. If what people say is true, that they are properly married, and that their union has been blessed by Pere Vincent the missioner, there is no harm in all that goes on between them, either in public or in private" ('Requete civile contre la Conclusion de la Paix, 1649).

The Man in the Iron Mask told the apothecary in the Bastille that he thought he was about sixty years of age ('Questions sur d'Encyclopedie'). Thus he must have been born in 1644, just at the time when Anne of Austria was invested with the royal power, though it was really exercised by Mazarin.

Can we find any incident recorded in history which lends support to the supposition that Anne of Austria had a son whose birth was kept as secret as her marriage to Mazarin?

"In 1644, Anne of Austria being dissatisfied with her apartments in the Louvre, moved to the Palais Royal, which had been left to the king by Richelieu. Shortly after taking up residence there she was very ill with a severe attack of jaundice, which was caused, in the opinion of the doctors, by worry, anxiety, and overwork, and which pulled her down greatly" ('Memoire de Madame de Motteville, 4 vols. 12mo, Vol i. p. 194).

"This anxiety, caused by the pressure of public business, was most probably only dwelt on as a pretext for a pretended attack of illness. Anne of Austria had no cause for worry and anxiety till 1649. She did not begin to complain of the despotism of Mazarin till towards the end of 1645" (Ibid., viol. i. pp. 272, 273).

"She went frequently to the theatre during her first year of widowhood, but took care to hide herself from view in her box." (Ibid., vol. i. p. 342).

Abbe Soulavie, in vol. vi. of the 'Memoires de Richelieu', published in 1793, controverted the opinions of M. de Saint-Mihiel, and again advanced those which he had published some time before, supporting them by a new array of reasons.

The fruitlessness of research in the archives of the Bastille, and the importance of the political events which were happening, diverted the attention of the public for some years from this subject. In the year 1800, however, the 'Magazin encyclopedique' published (vol. vi. p. 472) an article entitled 'Memoires sur les Problemes historiques, et la methode de les resoudre appliquee a celui qui concerne l'Homme au Masque de Fer', signed C. D. O., in which the author maintained that the prisoner was the first minister of the Duke of Mantua, and says his name was Girolamo Magni.

In the same year an octavo volume of 142 pages was produced by M. Roux-Fazillac. It bore the title 'Recherches historiques et critiques sur l'Homme au Masque de Fer, d'ou resultent des Notions certaines sur ce prisonnier'. These researches brought to light a secret correspondence relative to certain negotiations and intrigues, and to the abduction of a secretary of the Duke of Mantua whose name was Matthioli, and not Girolamo Magni.

In 1802 an octavo pamphlet containing 11 pages, of

which the author was perhaps Baron Lerviere, but which was signed Reth, was published. It took the form of a letter to General Jourdan, and was dated from Turin, and gave many details about Matthioli and his family. It was entitled 'Veritable Clef de l'Histoire de l'Homme au Masque de Fer'. It proved that the secretary of the Duke of Mantua was carried off, masked, and imprisoned, by order of Louis XIV in 1679, but it did not succeed in establishing as an undoubted fact that the secretary and the Man in the Iron Mask were one and the same person.

It may be remembered that M. Crawfurd writing in 1798 had said in his 'Histoire de la Bastille' (8vo, 474 pages), "I cannot doubt that the Man in the Iron Mask was the son of Anne of Austria, but am unable to decide whether he was a twin-brother of Louis XIV or was born while the king and queen lived apart, or during her widowhood." M. Crawfurd, in his 'Melanges d'Histoire et de Litterature tires dun Portefeuille' (quarto 1809, octavo 1817), demolished the theory advanced by Roux-Fazillac.

In 1825, M. Delort discovered in the archives several letters relating to Matthioli, and published his Histoire de l'Homme au Masque de Fer (8vo). This work was translated into English by George Agar-Ellis, and retranslated into French in 1830, under the title 'Histoire authentique du Prisonnier d'Etat, connu sons le Nom de Masque de Fer'. It is in this work that the suggestion is made that the captive was the second son of Oliver Cromwell.

In 1826, M. de Taules wrote that, in his opinion, the

masked prisoner was none other than the Armenian Patriarch. But six years later the great success of my drama at the Odeon converted nearly everyone to the version of which Soulavie was the chief exponent. The bibliophile Jacob is mistaken in asserting that I followed a tradition preserved in the family of the Duc de Choiseul; M. le Duc de Bassano sent me a copy made under his personal supervision of a document drawn up for Napoleon, containing the results of some researches made by his orders on the subject of the Man in the Iron Mask. The original MS., as well as that of the Memoires du Duc de Richelieu, were, the duke told me, kept at the Foreign Office. In 1834 the journal of the Institut historique published a letter from M. Auguste Billiard, who stated that he had also made a copy of this document for the late Comte de Montalivet, Home Secretary under the Empire.

M. Dufey (de l'Yonne) gave his 'Histoire de la Bastille' to the world in the same year, and was inclined to believe that the prisoner was a son of Buckingham.

Besides the many important personages on whom the famous mask had been placed, there was one whom everyone had forgotten, although his name had been put forward by the minister Chamillart: this was the celebrated Superintendent of Finance, Nicolas Fouquet. In 1837, Jacob, armed with documents and extracts, once more occupied himself with this Chinese puzzle on which so much ingenuity had been lavished, but of which no one had as yet got all the pieces into their places. Let us see if he succeeded better than his forerunners.

The first feeling he awakes is one of surprise. It seems odd that he should again bring up the case of Fouquet, who was condemned to imprisonment for life in 1664, confined in Pignerol under the care of Saint-Mars, and whose death was announced (falsely according to Jacob) on March 23rd, 1680. The first thing to look for in trying to get at the true history of the Mask is a sufficient reason of state to account for the persistent concealment of the prisoner's features till his death; and next, an explanation of the respect shown him by Louvois, whose attitude towards him would have been extraordinary in any age, but was doubly so during the reign of Louis XIV, whose courtiers would have been the last persons in the world to render homage to the misfortunes of a man in disgrace with their master. Whatever the real motive of the king's anger against Fouquet may have been, whether Louis thought he arrogated to himself too much power, or aspired to rival his master in the hearts of some of the king's mistresses, or even presumed to raise his eyes higher still, was not the utter ruin, the lifelong captivity, of his enemy enough to satiate the vengeance of the king? What could he desire more? Why should his anger, which seemed slaked in 1664, burst forth into hotter flames seventeen years later, and lead him to inflict a new punishment? According to the bibliophile, the king being wearied by the continual petitions for pardon addressed to him by the superintendent's family, ordered them to be told that he was dead, to rid himself of their supplications. Colbert's hatred, says he, was the immediate cause of Fouquet's fall; but even if this hatred hastened the catastrophe, are we to suppose that it pursued the delinquent beyond the sentence, through the long years of captivity, and, renewing its energy, infected the minds of the king and his councillors? If that were so, how shall we explain the respect shown by Louvois? Colbert would not have stood uncovered before Fouquet in prison. Why should Colbert's colleague have done so?

It must, however, be confessed that of all existing theories, this one, thanks to the unlimited learning and research of the bibliophile, has the greatest number of documents with the various interpretations thereof, the greatest profusion of dates, on its side.

For it is certain—

1st, that the precautions taken when Fouquet was sent to Pignerol resembled in every respect those employed later by the custodians of the Iron Mask, both at the Iles Sainte-Marguerite and at the Bastille;

2nd, that the majority of the traditions relative to the masked prisoner might apply to Fouquet;

3rd, that the Iron Mask was first heard of immediately after the announcement of the death of Fouquet in 1680;

4th, that there exists no irrefragable proof that Fouquet's death really occurred in the above year.

The decree of the Court of justice, dated 20th December 1664, banished Fouquet from the kingdom for life. "But the king was of the opinion that it would be dangerous to let the said Fouquet leave the country, in consideration of his intimate knowledge of the most important matters of state. Consequently the sentence of perpetual banishment was commuted into that of perpetual imprisonment." ('Receuil des defenses de M. Fouquet'). The instructions signed by the king and remitted to Saint-Mars forbid him to permit Fouquet to hold any spoken or written communication with anyone whatsoever, or to leave his apartments for any cause, not even for exercise. The great mistrust felt by Louvois pervades all his letters to Saint-Mars. The precautions which he ordered to be kept up were quite as stringent as in the case of the Iron Mask.

The report of the discovery of a shirt covered with writing, by a friar, which Abbe Papon mentions, may perhaps be traced to the following extracts from two letters written by Louvois to Saint-Mars: "Your letter has come to hand with the new handkerchief on which M. Fouquet has written" (18th Dec. 1665); "You can tell him that if he continues too employ his table-linen as note-paper he must not be surprised if you refuse to supply him with any more" (21st Nov. 1667).

Pere Papon asserts that a valet who served the masked prisoner died in his master's room. Now the man who waited on Fouquet, and who like him was sentenced to lifelong imprisonment, died in February 1680 (see letter of Louvois to Saint-Mars, 12th March 1680). Echoes of incidents which took place at Pignerol might have reached the Iles Sainte-Marguerite when Saint-Mars transferred his "former prisoner" from one fortress to the other. The fine clothes and linen, the books, all those luxuries in fact that were lavished on the masked prisoner, were not withheld from Fouquet. The furniture of a second room at Pignerol cost over 1200 livres (see letters of Louvois, 12th Dec. 1665, and 22nd Feb, 1666).

It is also known that until the year 1680 Saint-Mars had only two important prisoners at Pignerol, Fouquet and Lauzun. However, his "former prisoner of Pignerol," according to Du Junca's diary, must have reached the latter fortress before the end of August 1681, when Saint-Mars went to Exilles as governor. So that it was in the interval between the 23rd March 1680, the alleged date of Fouquet's death, and the 1st September 1681, that the Iron Mask appeared at Pignerol, and yet Saint-Mars took only two prisoners to Exilles. One of these was probably the Man in the Iron Mask; the other, who must have been Matthioli, died before the year 1687, for when Saint-Mars took over the governorship in the month of January of that year of the Iles Sainte-Marguerite he brought only ONE prisoner thither with him. "I have taken such good measures to guard my prisoner that I can answer to you for his safety" ('Lettres de Saint-Mars a Louvois', 20th January 1687).

In the correspondence of Louvois with Saint-Mars we find, it is true, mention of the death of Fouquet on March 23rd, 1680, but in his later correspondence Louvois never says "the late M. Fouquet," but speaks of him, as usual, as "M. Fouquet" simply. Most historians have given as a fact that Fouquet was interred in the same vault as his father in the chapel of Saint-Francois de Sales in the convent church belonging to the Sisters of the Order of the Visitation-Sainte-Marie, founded in the beginning of the seventeenth century by Madame de Chantal. But proof to the contrary exists; for the subterranean portion of St. Francis's chapel was closed in 1786, the last person interred there being Adelaide Felicite Brulard, with whom ended the house of Sillery. The convent was shut up in 1790, and the church given over to the Protestants in 1802; who continued to respect the tombs. In 1836 the Cathedral chapter of Bourges claimed the remains of one of their archbishops buried there in the time of the Sisters of Sainte-Marie. On this occasion all the coffins were examined and all the inscriptions carefully copied, but the name of Nicolas Fouquet is absent.

Voltaire says in his 'Dictionnaire philosophique', article "Ana," "It is most remarkable that no one knows where the celebrated Fouquet was buried."

But in spite of all these coincidences, this carefully constructed theory was wrecked on the same point on which the theory that the prisoner was either the Duke of Monmouth or the Comte de Vermandois came to grief, viz. a letter from Barbezieux, dated 13th August 1691, in which occur the words, "THE PRISONER WHOM YOU HAVE HAD IN CHARGE FOR TWENTY YEARS." According to this testimony, which Jacob had successfully used against his predecessors, the prisoner referred to could not have been Fouquet, who completed his twenty-seventh year of captivity in 1691, if still alive.

We have now impartially set before our readers all the

opinions which have been held in regard to the solution of this formidable enigma. For ourselves, we hold the belief that the Man in the Iron Mask stood on the steps of the throne. Although the mystery cannot be said to be definitely cleared up, one thing stands out firmly established among the mass of conjecture we have collected together, and that is, that wherever the prisoner appeared he was ordered to wear a mask on pain of death. His features, therefore, might during half a century have brought about his recognition from one end of France to the other; consequently, during the same space of time there existed in France a face resembling the prisoner's known through all her provinces, even to her most secluded isle.

Whose face could this be, if not that of Louis XVI, twin-brother of the Man in the Iron Mask?

To nullify this simple and natural conclusion strong evidence will be required.

Our task has been limited to that of an examining judge at a trial, and we feel sure that our readers will not be sorry that we have left them to choose amid all the conflicting explanations of the puzzle. No consistent narrative that we might have concocted would, it seems to us, have been half as interesting to them as to allow them to follow the devious paths opened up by those who entered on the search for the heart of the mystery. Everything connected with the masked prisoner arouses the most vivid curiosity. And what end had we in view? Was it not to denounce a crime and to brand the perpetrator thereof? The facts as they stand are sufficient for our object, and speak more eloquently than if used to adorn a tale or to prove an ingenious theory.

www.ingramcontent.com/pod-product-compliance
Lightning Source LLC
LaVergne TN
LVHW041309080426
835510LV00009B/921